River of Tears

River of Tears

Maud Emery

drawings by Rudi Lang

hancock house

ISBN 0-88839-276-1
Copyright © 1992 Maud Emery

Cataloging in Publication Data
Emery, Maud
River of tears

ISBN 0-88839-276-1

1. Cariboo (B.C.: Regional district)—Gold discoveries—Fiction. 2. Massacres—British Columbia—Fiction. 3. Tsilkotin Indians—Wars—Fiction. 4. Indians of North America—British Columbia—Wars—Fiction. 5. Indians of North America—Canada—Wars—1814-1885—Fiction.* I. Title.
PS8559.M47R5 1992   C813'.54   C89-091015-4
PR9199.3.E55R5 1992

All rights reserved. No part of this publication may be reproduced, stored in a retrieval system or transmitted, in any form or by any means, electronic, mechanical, photocopying, recording or otherwise, without the prior written permission of Hancock House Publishers.

Printed in Hong Kong

Published simultaneously in Canada and the United States by

HANCOCK HOUSE PUBLISHERS LTD.
19313 Zero Avenue, Surrey, B.C. V4P 1M7

HANCOCK HOUSE PUBLISHERS
1431 Harrison Avenue, Blaine, WA 98230

Contents

	Dedication	6
	Prolog	7
1	Cheela	9
2	Bute Inlet	15
3	Piele	22
4	Talapus the Wolf	28
5	On Waddington's Crew	36
6	Squint Eye's News	42
7	Cheela and Piele	47
8	The Massacre	54
9	The Hunt	63
10	Reflections	69
11	The Trial	73
12	Shadows	79
13	The Execution	84
14	Cheela	89
	Epilog	95
	Further Reading	96

Dedicated

To

Truth
Justice
and Honor

Prolog

The recorded history of the Chilcotin War (the Bute Inlet massacre) is somewhat meager in many details, and often sources are contradictory. The author has therefore endeavored to weave an accurate life pattern of the Indians, and white people, of the time — early 1860s — using provincial archives and the historical files of *The Colonist* newspaper in Victoria as primary sources. Historians disagree on the number of Indians involved, the exact reasons for the their attack on the whites, the number of whites killed, and the number of survivors. They vary in their versions of the chase, capture, and execution of the Indians. So the author has chosen what sounds like the most likely version of events for the setting of this very human story, as supported by the greatest number of sources.

The author has interlaced the lives of fictional characters, based on research of the Coast Salish and Chilcotin peoples, with some of the major players in the Bute Island massacre, whose roles she also researched — from many sources.

The resulting "novelette" is thus firmly planted in the roots of British Columbia history, yet poignantly portrays the effects of a brutal slaughter on the lives of one family. Mother and wife reflect the hopes, the way of life, and the anguish of those times. (As the primary interest is to reflect their point of view, certain liberties have been taken.)

1
Cheela

It was colder than usual on the banks of the Homathko River, as the dark glacial water flowed solemnly to the sea. From mountain peaks and ice fields, through canyoned walls of stone, the river tumbled into Waddington Harbor at the head of Bute Inlet.

If measuring time in the white man's way, the month was October, and the year was 1861.

The two Indian women sat in their hut beside the river. The young woman called Cheela was speaking to take their minds off the cold and their loneliness. She looked down at the child she cradled in her arms.

"Winter will come early, and the wind will bring snow and ice," Cheela warned.

Then she told her son Toko the story of the Salmon People, who had escaped the land of the wind by living beneath the sea. But before her story ended, some primitive terror seized her and she clasped the boy and held him close, clinging to him as though fearing the wind or some evil spirit would snatch him from her.

There were tears streaming down the brown and wrinkled face of the old Indian woman, Miska. Even a good story could not make her smile anymore, thought Cheela. Old Miska was very sad these days.

Toko, thinking of the Salmon People, fell asleep in Cheela's arms.

Cheela knew this year winter was coming early, beginning with rain and high winds that would strip the hillsides of their russet leaves — their red and golden gowns — and scatter them like tattered rags upon the cold, damp earth.

Cheela and Miska sat in their silent home made of earth, brush, and bark. Like the leaves, the two women had once been bright and full of happiness, and had danced upon the summer's wind. Now they sat motionless and lifeless as the glacial winds rattled the crude door of the lonely hut on the edge of the river.

Cheela's eyes focused on the small stone lying in the corner of the hut; it was a stone that she had collected a long time ago, on the creek called the Cumsack. It contained the brightest glints of mica that she had ever seen. She had hunted and hunted the creek, and the river, and the beach, for others like it, but she had never found one.

Cheela stared at the stone as if hypnotized, but her mind began to wander elsewhere. She thought of her husband Piele and wished he'd return soon from his hunting trip at Tatlayoko Lake.

And she wished the old woman Miska would cease weeping. It was useless to remember what had happened. It was over and done with; there was nothing they could do about it. The hurt would always be with them. It was better, her father had often reminded her as a child, to bend, like a tree, to the wind; to go with the current; to follow the fish, to follow the deer.

But Miska was old, and not always feeling well. She cried easily, and often, these days.

Cheela stared at the stone as if she could see her past in it. She saw her face in the stone. She had been young and pretty when she'd met Piele. Her face had been round, with soft, dark eyes. Her hair was dark too, blacker than her eyes, and it hung in a thick braid down her back.

Cheela recalled the time when she had found the stone at Cumsack Creek, the place where she had been born and lived until she had met Piele.

When the leaves had begun to turn brilliant reds and yellows, and the winds were still light, her family had traveled across the head of Bute Inlet, to Miimaya, the place where her people met other peoples to harvest and smoke and dry fish for winter storage.

Cheela was only a few moons past her time of seclusion then. All summer she had slept apart from her family's sleeping area. She had eaten little and drunk little. She had touched nothing, nor looked at anyone. For Cheela — like all girls in their time of puberty — had the power to spoil things. She could not touch the berry bush, for all the fruits would turn black. She could not touch the beach, for all the clams would disappear. Her hair was tied in a knot at the back of her head, and if she had touched it, she would have gone bald. She rubbed her hairline with a special wet stone to make her hair grow long and healthy. She had her face painted with a mixture of burned stinging nettles and charcoal. There had been bands of the inner bark of the red cedar tied around her wrists and ankles.

All of this training had been to make Cheela more eligible for marriage. She had been glad when the *season of the sun,* summer, ended and she could travel across the inlet with her family and again look at others and speak to them.

The people of the young man's river, the Chilcotin, to the north and the east, had set up camp across the inlet, at Miimaya with her people. They, too, had needed to take salmon from the sea. More often than not, they traded goods with the coastal Indians for their fish and moved on. The Chilcotin people had learned much of their social ways and material values from Cheela's Salish people, though they remained fiercely proud. Here, at the village, Cheela had met Piele, who took her from the sea also.

There had been a great potlatch celebrating the joining of Piele and Cheela. It was not usual for Homathko girls to marry Chilcotin men, who were bold, restless, and often turbulent. But Piele's mother, Miska, was a Homathko Indian, and the time of intertribal wars was over. Piele, as soon as he was old enough, had left his mother, who had spent more time at the Bute Inlet village with her son than she had with her husband on the trail, as was the custom among his people. He had traveled up the Homathko to learn what he should from Klatsassin, a great Chilcotin chief. Many said this was because Piele was Klatsassin's son, Miska's restless husband.

Cheela had begun her life of wandering with Piele then, leaving behind the more settled life at Cumsack Creek. She and Piele led a carefree, nomadic life: camping, hunting, and fishing along the rivers and wandering through the mountains between the Chilco and Homathko.

At the time of her seclusion, Cheela had practiced a little magic. She had caught a small snake and dropped it down the front of her body. The snake quickly squirmed free of her; so Cheela knew all her babies would be born without complication. And it was not long before Cheela had given Piele three sons.

Three times the mama and the *chitish,* grandmother, had announced to Cheela's newborns, "you will be growing with the daylight," and all three children grew happy and healthy, growing a little more each time the sun rose over the mountains.

But now only little Toko, the last to be born, was left. Only Toko.

The first born, Tenas Pootie, was gone. Keeto, her second baby, had also gone away, with his brother, to the land of the dead.

The white man's plague had reached them at Tatlayoko Lake. Tenas Pootie and Keeto had become ill. They had cried, Cheela remembered, and whimpered that they were cold, so cold she could not keep them warm, no matter how many bear skins she wrapped around them. Then the chills changed to burning fevers, and the children began to vomit. For three days they had cried and vomited and burned with fever.

The old Miska had gone out herb gathering and brought back wild berry leaves, cascara bark, and Oregon grape root, which she boiled over the fire to create a rich drink. This drink had eased the thirst of their fevers, but it did not stop their faces and throats from swelling or prevent the hundreds of pustules from erupting all over their bodies. The blotches filled their nostrils and choked their throats until the children could no longer breathe or swallow, and Cheela could no longer get Miska's herbal drink into them.

Before long, Keeto's moaning, twisting, and crying ceased. Not too much later, Tenas Pootie turned over, and a gurgle of anguish came from his swollen throat. It was the last sound Tenas Pootie made.

Piele had launched his sons toward the spirit world, placing their mortuary boxes, like canoes on the river, in a sheltered grove near Tatlayoko Lake, his favorite hunting ground. He'd placed them high up in a pair of trees, wedging the little boxes into the crooks of solid branches with the trunks. It was not a time to carve mortuary poles, as some of Cheela's people sometimes did; but he chose their way of "burial," to honor them and Cheela, and his mother.

Piele had then taken his family away, away from the contagion that had spread, like fog, over Chilcotin and Tatlayoko country. Sickness was everywhere: in the air, in the trees, in the ground, in their food. There were Indian graves across the land.

Then Piele had heard that the scourge was lessening; so they'd returned to Homathko, where Piele thought they were safe.

The small stone came into focus again. That's all it was, Cheela sighed, a gray stone with bright flecks of gold in it. Cheela roused herself, looked across at the old Miska, who was quiet until she thought again of the plague.

Cheela wondered sometimes if the poor woman was filled with the white man's disease, the way Miska cried as the sun rose and set. It had been six moons since the boys had gone to the land of the dead, and still Miska cried harder than ever.

If only Piele would come, Cheela thought, for Miska always brightened when Piele was home. Perhaps he would shorten his hunting trip and return to Homathko. The sooner he came, the better for them all. She sat still. The Homathko wind blew down the river valley passed their humble hut.

2
Bute Inlet

Miska was old but her memory was long. She remembered standing with her people on the shores of Bute Inlet, as the white people call it, and seeing the floating island for the first time. It appeared in the inlet as if by magic, and it mystified her. And frightened her. The trees of this island were stripped of all their leaves — as if burned — and thrust barrenly upward into the great empty sky. Miska had gripped her mother's hand.

Then she watched as out of a little house on the floating islands and from under and around the "burned trees," and from everywhere on this island, came the pale strangers: men with white skin covered in dark fabrics which fitted their bodies. Their heads were topped with queer-shaped "hats."

"This great seabird," Miska's mother had said solemnly, "is far more powerful than Heron, Eagle, or even Raven."

Two canoes had left the shore and glided out to meet the floating island. Her father and the elders offered bows and arrows and, in return, received nails, pieces of iron, copper, beads, medals, and mirrors.

When Miska's father had returned, he handed her something that shone in the sunlight and reflected into Miska's eye. Miska never forgot the glint and the shine of that button. Never forgot her first experience of the fabled pale-skinned strangers who had been reported sighted by their southern neighbors for as long as she could remember. She never forgot the fear inside her, or her mother's words. Or how the pale men had floated in canoes around the inlet and put on stuff called paper what the inlet looked like. They did not bother her people. Yet...

After a few sunsets, the great bird-ship had pulled away from the inlet. All of this had been a vision weird and wonderful and terrifying for the small Miska, who sensed the fear and apprehension of the elders. She had felt the relief, the freedom, when the strange apparition was gone. The chief of the floating island had given orders for the heavy "anchor," a giant mud hook, to be raised, and for the wings to open, or the "sails to unfurl." The sky was clear and a favorable wind was blowing; the sails fluttered and filled, sending the vessel adrift and away.

Miska had watched the island sailing farther and farther away, growing smaller and smaller, until she couldn't see it at all.

The huge, supernatural seabird with the great white wings that had floated like an island into Bute Inlet was the companion ship of the *Discovery*. The two ships were sailing under the colors of Britain, under the command of the man they called Captain George Vancouver. And the "chief" of the companion ship, the *Chatham,* was James Johnstone. If measuring time as the white man does, the year was 1792.

But Miska knew none of that. She knew only the fear of foreboding.

After the ship had slipped into the horizon and disappeared as birds do into the sky, Miska searched with her mother for roots and bark for basket weaving. They would enjoy life as they always had, before the boat arrived. Miska had hidden the shiny button so that her cousin Chikatt could not take it from her. But as she grew older, the shiny object began to frighten her. She knew by instinct that the coming of this white-winged bird and these white-skinned men would haunt her all the days of her life.

At night, Miska would listen to Chikatt tell about his visions. Chikatt saw the strangest images when delirious with fever from eating poisoned berries. Chikatt knew better than to eat those berries, but Chikatt was like that. He never listened to others; he found out things for himself. Chikatt saw an animal with the body of the cougar and the heads of a wolf, a bear, and a serpent. The three-headed animal chased Chikatt out of his mind one night, as he lay in the lodge and screamed so the entire family heard him. Once Chikatt had seen a *mowitch,* a deer, with a coat of raven's feather's instead of fur. Chikatt could never be trusted with a bow and arrow. Once he shot it backward and nearly killed himself. Then there was the time of the three shining eyes in the forest. The eyes belonged to the red cedar who went out every night looking for the man who'd taken bark from his trunk. When this man was found, the red cedar tree would bend over and crush him to death.

Chikatt the Crazy One they called him, because he had more visions than anyone in the village.

Miska began to wonder if she was affected with Chikatt's vision. Or if she had the power of her mother, to see into the future. That thought disturbed her and she shook her shoulders, as to throw it off.

The apparition in the inlet had been the biggest and finest constructed canoe she had seen. And its strange people had left her a link — the shiny button.

Miska recalled that her mother had warned her about the button and told Miska to bury it in the dark, rich sand at low tide. "You must be wary of that great bird. He is more powerful than even Raven."

As she'd said this, she had slid her bone needle into the sealskin moccasins she was making, as if she were driving the needle into the hide of the pale chief of the floating island.

"They'll be back," she'd warned.

Miska's mother had not lived to see the power of the white men. Miska had held her hand and stroked her hair and soothed her forehead as she lay dying.

And now Miska was an old woman too. Soon, it would be her time to go to that happy land beyond the trees and the sky, beyond her beloved Homathko. How she loved its towering mountains, its rivers, and its trees, the changing colors and seasons. And the wind. She watched it all, lovingly. The maple, alder, and cottonwood leaves turning red, crimson, and yellow each fall. The wild geese flying south; the ponds and creeks freezing solid; the distant glaciers appearing closer; the winds driving rain, sleet, and snow across the land and down the inlet. When the snow ceased, Miska heard the hush when nothing stirred. She had listened to the silence when death lay upon the land. All of these things she had known.

All this had been her home. Now it was changing. The white man had come. He was here. He was here to tame and use the land in his own way. He would harness the rivers, mow down their forests, chase away the wildlife, and empty the seas of their fish and the shores of their clams.

Miska did foresee all of this — in the shiny button — even as her mother had foreseen it. With the "sixth power" of her mother, Miska saw a settlement at the head of Bute Inlet. There were white men and white men's homes: cabins and shacks and lodges. This vision haunted her for several days; then it disappeared as suddenly as it had come.

This vision was not without foundation. In the future, in the white man's year of 1895, surveyors would arrive in Bute Inlet and map out a townsite. There would be homesteads, too. A few miles from the mouth of the Homathko River, pioneers would settle. The white men would build a school, a lodge, a general store, a hall, and a church; shacks, cabins, and houses, made mostly of logs. A few would clear the land to farm, put up shelters, and plant potatoes. Every two weeks a steamer would arrive with mail and supplies. Speculators from Victoria would buy up townsite lots, and the cash register at the general store would ring with prosperity. Even Miska's people would take advantage of the arrival of the white men: the skin of a bear would sell for many days' pay in the white man's money in 1895. Other Indians would offer logs to the white men in exchange for stuff called tea, flour, sugar, bacon, and other supplies used by the white man.

The store would boom, a hotel too, as prospectors, land speculators, and gamblers arrived. In the evening, the community hall would be bright with lamps and lanterns, with dances, songs, recitations, and suppers.

They would come, as Miska envisioned, but they would not stay. Bute Inlet's boom was to be short-lived. The town would sink almost as fast as it would rise. In a few years, it would have faded into history, and Bute Inlet would be given back to the wilderness. And the wind.

The wind. Miska's mother had told her of the wind. "Our people have always lived here, and the wind has always blown," her mother had said. Then she'd told Miska the story of Raven and Wind-maker and how the winds came to be.

Once, there was a very strong wind blowing. Raven and the others were getting tired of the strong wind, as they were unable to travel. Raven, Heron, Seagull, and Grebe held a meeting to find out where the wind was coming from. Thinking it was coming from the North, they headed off on that course.

Seagull, who was top-heavy, had a hard time traveling. Finally, they all had to stop, because of the wind. This made Raven very angry. He was so angry he wanted to kill whoever was making this wind.

Finally they managed to carry on, and they reached the northern country where Wind-maker lived with his wife and young boy. Raven and the others knew this was where the wind was coming from. The people didn't have clothes in those days, and they noticed that Wind-maker's ribs were starting to ripple — he was going to make the wind blow.

"It is strange that you don't kill him," Heron said to the others. Then he ran straight at Wind-maker, ramming through his stomach with his sharp beak. Wind-maker died. Heron ran after the woman and killed her too.

"We will keep the boy as a slave," Raven told Heron. "We won't kill him."

They started traveling back home, but on the way the little boy's ribs began to ripple as he lay in the canoe. The wind began to blow and they had to head for shore. So Raven started to pound on the boy's stomach. The rippling of his ribs subsided, and immediately the wind died down, too. Now Raven knew for sure where the wind was coming from.

Yet Raven did not kill the boy. He took him home, although they had to stop several times along the way to pound the boy's stomach.

Today, there are many winds because Raven took Wind-maker's boy home with him.

3
Piele

Piele returned early as Cheela had hoped, bringing with him skins to be cured and meat to be smoked.

Miska was proud of her son Piele, her second, who had grown into a fine young man. Piele had learned well the lessons that made an Indian strong and brave. Chief Klatsassin had seen to that. Klatsassin had taught Piele to hunt and fish, to be honest and proud. Klatsassin and the wilderness had shaped Piele. The wilderness of rivers, lakes, mountains, and trackless forests had created him. Campfires, alder smoke, pine, and balsam scent were the breath of Piele's being. The mighty Homathko wind blew in his soul. He loved the land as much as did his mother Miska.

Piele picked up little Toko and hugged him. Cheela and Miska's eyes followed Piele, asking the question their tongues could not. He understood. Yes, he told them, he'd been to the graves. They were as he had left them, when he first "buried" Tenas Pootie and Keeto.

Piele would never forget the day he had walked away from Tatlayoko Lake, leaving his sons. He had washed them and combed their hair, bound them in a crouching position: knees close to their heads, arms

wrapped around their legs, hands under their feet. He had wrapped the boys in new blankets and placed them in boxes hewn from cedar. All this he did in the manner of his mother's people, who were Cheela's people, the people who had raised him. After placing the closed boxes safely in the trees, wedged firmly between solid branches and the tree trunks, Piele had burned Tenas Pootie's and Keeto's miniature hunting tools and fishing hooks so the boys could use them in the land of the dead.

Piele had stood beside the graves long after the smoldering embers had died. He stood a long time remembering many things. The health, strength, youth, and laughter of these children who had vanished into the silence. They had gone to the playground beyond the stars, the sun, the sky, and the wind. But the scourge that had killed his boys, and boys—and whole families—of his people and of the peoples all around . . . had *that* left the land? The scourge that had been unknown to his people before the coming of the white man.

It had been six moons since he'd "buried" his sons, but Piele knew he would never forget them, or the hundreds of other graves across the land. Weeds, bracken, alder saplings, and bush were already growing over the rocks and beneath the burial boxes, but nothing could ever grow over and around Piele's heart to dull the pain he felt there.

Now, though, he was home. Cheela and Miska and Toko needed him. He would stay with them for a time, before he left to see his friend and teacher Klatsassin. The two men were planning to go to the hills and swamps along the Chilco and upper Homathko rivers to hunt. It was the time just as the snow began to fly and the caribou would be waiting. They were going to camp in Tatlayoko Lake country, where the water was good and game was plentiful, and near where he'd launched Tenas Pootie and Keeto into their spirit world.

Now, Piele suggested they all go to the inlet to visit Cheela's people and dig clams. They would talk and laugh and forget their heartaches, and think of better days ahead. There would be ceremonies, and dancing, and a clambake. Both Cheela and Miska could return to where they had come from.

Cheela smiled. Perhaps she would hear news of her brother, the one they called Talapus the Wolf. She had heard nothing of him for such a long time. But then, Talapus was like that, never staying in one place for long. The last time she'd heard of him, he was at Kyoquot, on the shores of the big water, the Pacific Ocean, on what people now called Vancouver's Island. Some said that Talapus had married a white girl, a daughter of a missionary. Despite the missionary's teachings of brotherly love, it was said that he did not approve of his daughter, his *tenas klootchman,* marrying an Indian. They said Talapus had left with his bride for Victoria, and that was the last Cheela had heard of her brother. She often wondered where he was, and if she would see him again. News of Talapus at this time would help ease the ache that was inside her. She yearned to touch her roots.

Miska, hearing Piele and Cheela talk of their plans, shook her head. She knew, just as she knew when rain or a storm was on the way, or when the Homathko wind had changed, or when snow would come, that troubled times were ahead. She knew by the ache in her bones. But Piele and Cheela were facing up to life, facing the loss of their sons. She would not burden them with her own visions. She would remain silent. She would go with them to Cumsack Creek and help them dig clams. She would have a real feast on clams again. It would be good. She would gather herbs and roots which did not grow in the colder region of Homathko. Miska would visit the elders at Cumsack Creek, old women like herself, who would take her to a shaman to rid her of her evils. He would mix up a special potion for her to drink. By doing his magic, he would scare away the spirits that were troubling her.

Miska would be glad to get away from all that haunted her here. She did not get this feeling anywhere else, which meant that trouble—when it came—would be in Homathko. She knew trouble was on the way.

But she wouldn't spoil the new mood by saying anything. Let them enjoy this happy time.

Even as Miska and her old bones traveled with her family down the river to Cumsack Creek, though, more ships were arriving in far-off inlets, and wagons and horses were creaking across trails through the mountains. Explorers, adventurers, fortune seekers, miners, and laborers spilled across the land which had been Miska's grandfather's. A few pale newcomers also traveled on foot, their possessions in sacks slung over their shoulders.

The discovery of gold in the Cariboo country, which the world had learned about in the white man's year of 1858, had caused a rush of men to the goldfields. Gold! It was the stuff that lured white men to madness and murder. Some of them murdered some Indians. Some of them hired Indians and some of those cheated some of "their" Indians, packtrain guides and packers. The precious metal was the golden-haired siren that drew men to rivers, creeks, and mines with the promise of wealth. In addition to miners, there were businessmen, gamblers, investors, and brokers, all looking for a stake or a steal in the haul. In spite of the Indian people.

News of gold in the Cariboo country (in Barkerville) and in the Chilcotin had spread, over the years, north, south, east, and west. The call was heard and they came, as Miska's mother had predicted they would; they came from all directions into Miska's country. Among them was a man named Alfred Penderill Waddington, who would eventually stumble upon Piele's and Cheela's home ground and cause more tears to flood Miska's aging eyes. As if to prepare for that, the Wind-maker's ribs rippled, and the old Homathko wind sighed through the trees.

4
Talapus the Wolf

Talapus, brother to the wandering wolf and the brother of Cheela, had been born with restless feet. He could not stay tied to a place, a calendar, or a clock, and eventually the missionary's daughter from Kyoquot had given up on Talapus, who would not stay tethered. She had shackled Talapus the Wolf with a foreign marriage ceremony but she'd failed to shackle his feet.

"I'm very sorry," Alfred Waddington said to Talapus.

Talapus was telling Waddington the story of his marriage as he dipped his paddle through the clear water. Talapus was showing the man the intricate inlets and waterways east of Victoria and how to navigate them by watching the ripples in the currents. Waddington had offered him supplies, glass jars full of shiny nails and buttons among them, if Talapus could show him how to slide the canoe effortlessly through the waters.

The strange pair had met under unusual circumstances and were somehow drawn to each other through a bond of sympathy.

The day had been an unhappy one for Talapus. His cousin, Allache, had just been hanged for murdering a young man, whom he'd warned often enough to keep away from his wife. Talapus, like the wolf, had heard the news on the wind, and had traveled to the big island the white man had named after the fabled Captain Vancouver, and found the spot in that island's great city called Victoria where they were hanging Allache.

Talapus, through his grief, was moved by the anger being expressed to a small crowd by the big white man. Talapus had spoken to him, telling him that Allache had been his cousin.

"He was never given a fair trial," the man said.

The man was Alfred Waddington, and he and Talapus, feeling a mystical tugging toward each other, talked for hours.

"Come with me," Waddington had invited. "We'll talk some more, and you will feel better."

From that day on, Talapus the Wolf became friend, then confidant and advisor, to this white man with a vision.

"I am worried about the fate of Victoria and its merchants," Waddington confessed.

And he spoke of turning the little village of 800 people into a real town, with streets and hotels and stores.

"Why?" asked Talapus.

"Gold, Talapus, that's why. There's gold in the Fraser River, gold at Williams Creek, gold at Barkerville. Miners are pouring into Victoria on their way to the goldfields. Victoria should be prepared for this and the prosperity that will follow.

"People are getting to the goldfields by New Westminster and they are passing us by."

Talapus saw nothing wrong with things the way they were. White people got funny ideas sometimes. Waddington's worries had much to do with money, and of shiny buttons in glass jars. Talapus did not yearn for money, but for the white man's trinkets, and his exciting but frightening talk, he did not mind slipping around islands and further exploring the ocean currents.

Waddington spoke of crazy things, unheard of things. White men were like that. Talapus the Wolf listened attentively but in bewilderment. His new friend's enthusiasm made him nervous. Waddington wanted Talapus to be involved in his schemes. But Talapus didn't want to get involved in anything that might curb his freedom. After *too* much talk, Talapus felt he should be moving along, and glided the canoe to the Songhies Point in Victoria Harbor.

Waddington made him promise that he would return soon.

Talapus did return, and he listened to more of Waddington's plans. But in time, Talapus's feet became restless again.

One day he told Waddington he was going back to Cumsack Creek in Bute Inlet to see his people, and perhaps go farther north to find his sister, Cheela. At the mention of Bute Inlet, for Talapus has used the white man's place names, Waddington became excited.

"Bute Inlet?"

"Sure," Talapus answered. "My home. But I move around. They call me the Wolf. Like the wolf I travel by night and I travel by day. I even howl at the moon sometimes. Ha."

"How far away is Bute Inlet?" Waddington inquired.

"My canoe goes through water like the scared seal. Talapus the Wolf goes like a swish." His arm swept through the air.

"That fast?"

Talapus laughed. "Or I take my time, depends on how I feel. Sometimes Talapus lazy, sometimes weather bad. Some bad winds can blow, then it's hard to travel. But I get there."

Waddington persuaded Talapus to stay a while and hear him out: to listen to more plans, more wild schemes, to endorse and encourage his enthusiasm. Talapus listened to Waddington's dreams that would make Victoria and Bute Inlet famous and miners and himself rich.

Soon after, Talapus departed on his long canoe journey to Bute Inlet. His aimless, drifting approach to life seemed always to steer him through currents that knew when and where to come and go at the most opportune moments. That Talapus should arrive at Cumsack Creek in his canoe just as Cheela and Piele came down the crest of the last hillside was an example of the luck that so often came Talapus's way.

Cheela's delight at seeing him again was like a magic potion for her recent sorrows. Piele, too, was cheered by the presence of Talapus and was anxious to hear his news.

Talapus had much news to tell them. He had a canoeful of news. There were good times ahead for Bute Inlet. Waddington had talked to the "Big Chief" of the white men, the governor, in Victoria. He had permission called a charter and he was going to build a wagon road from the head of Bute Inlet through to the Chilcotin/Cariboo gold. People would pay to use Waddington's road. Waddington would get rich, and the Indians would get rich.

"How will we get rich?" Piele asked Talapus.

"He will give me and my people jobs and make us rich," Talapus explained. "With my friend Waddington in charge, we will be given much."

"But how will he get a road through the mountains, rocks, canyons, and forests between Homathko and Chilcotin?" they asked.

"I explained to him about the land," Talapus answered. "But he will not listen. He tells me white men can do this."

Few believed him. But Talapus the Wolf did not give a wag of his bushy tail whether it could be done or not. He would have drifted off to some other place by the time a road was ever built in Bute Inlet. Talapus knew everyone had a dream of some sort inside him, and if others' dreams didn't interfere with his own dream of always being on the move, it was fine with him.

"He is crazy," Talapus's people said of the white man Waddington. To build a road through mountains of solid rock, a road to cross steep canyons and rushing rivers . . . surely he would need some extraordinary power to do that.

That brother of hers, Cheela thought. He was a smart one. He moved about, heard things, knew what was going on with the white men.

"You are crazy," she teased him, and they laughed together.

Later, Talapus's moccasins took him away from her again. Who knows where? He was just gone. But Cheela had had the comfort of once again touching her roots.

When the birds appeared in the sky in the *sun go away moon* time, the time that was spring to the white man in the year of 1862, Talapus's Waddington arrived

with a crew of seventy men and a big boat they called a ferry loaded with foodstuffs and supplies. The summer passed and the landscape changed. Twenty-three of the white man's miles, in a ribbon they called a road, emerged on the horizon, ten feet wide. Sixty-five single-span bridges had been constructed across crevices along the trail; one bridge reached ninety feet. Big thunder, called explosives, threw trees and boulders aside to make way.

The white man had indeed brought an extraordinary power to move the Creator's trees. It took the spirit of the trees from them. And the Chilcotin and Homathko workers who had hired on to help, as Talapus had said they would, were frightened and awed by this power of the white man.

The Indians did the white man's bidding, partly out of this awe, and partly because this was simply the new way, although sometimes the white man boss was not kind. He did not respect the Homathko way or the Chilcotin tradition. They did not "worship" the spirit of the tree.

The months and seasons passed. Then it was *elder moon*. Work shut down for the season of snow. When *sun go away moon* returned, the white man saw what was expected of him in this land. Ten of the bridges had been swept away, and seven others were damaged by winter's ice and the early spring floods.

The white men, the Indians said, do not understand Homathko. They do not know about the winds. They do not know that *Xwemalhkwu,* the name of the Homathko River, means "swift water." They do not take their lessons from Mother Earth with the stoic patience of the Homathkos or the understanding shrug of the Chilcotin.

So Waddington's crew returned to work and the trail began again, this time bypassing the river canyon. This was something Talapus's people had not expected. That man Waddington was determined. As

Talapus had said, you had to admire a man like that, even if he was crazy in the head. Piele agreed. Cheela watched in awe. Miska wept in alarm. Talapus was not surprised when he saw it. He felt the restless Homathko wind in his soul as the wind stirred and rippled the sheltered river's water.

5

On Waddington's Crew

As suddenly as he had merged into the disappearing landscape, Talapus reemerged. He met Piele and Cheela at Tatlayoko Lake, where they had gone with their little, nomadic family to gather early roots and edible shoots. They persuaded Talapus to come back with them to Homathko. Talapus was happy to be with his sister again, and, besides, he would be close enough to watch the development of Waddington's road.

Waddington was up against a wall of trouble: to push a road through country filled with ravines, yawning chasms, and towering mountains was as tough as Talapus had warned Waddington it would be. But it would take more than snow, floods, and bridge washouts to deter Waddington.

By early spring of this second year of construction, the time of early root picking, in the white man's year of 1863, Waddington's crew was back on the job, determined to finish the road. Among them was a man named Brewster, appointed by Waddington as superintendent of the construction crews. Brewster hired a number of Chilcotin Indians as packers and laborers, and a burly fellow by the name of Biggs as foreman.

They needed help to rebuild the road and to continue on from there.

Talapus and Piele discussed joining up for a job. Talapus thought it would suit him for a time, until his feet again got the traveling urge. Piele thought there might be something in it for him. He'd seen the scowloads and packtrains of tools, implements — shovels, axes, buckets, cooking pots — that were being brought in, things that he and Cheela could use. He saw the food supplies the white man used. He saw things that could make their lives, Cheela's and Miska's and Toko's and his own, a little easier. He saw that payment for work was sometimes made with trinkets and beads, sometimes with blankets, other times in the white man's currency, money. Sometimes, too, payment was made in the form of the white man's thunderstick, the rifle. With ammunition. That, he'd seen, made hunting easier.

Piele, the Chilcotin, applied for a job as packer. Brewster took him on. Piele was young, strong, pleasant, and friendly. Brewster liked him. Then Talapus applied for a job, and Brewster also took him on. Soon, Piele moved Cheela, little Toko, and old Miska up the valley, closer to the work sites, and he and Talapus built them a second hut on the banks of the Homathko River.

Cheela's people had always fished, hunted, and lived in harmony with the mountains and water. They shared trails in the forests with the Deer People and the Moose People without cutting away forests and erecting bridges.

But the newcomers were cutting down trees, digging up roots, splitting, sawing, hacking, hammering, nailing, shoveling — changing the face of the land, with fierce determination. They let nothing, and nobody, stop them. They even set off many explosions with their magic potion, that thing that was so destructive that dirt, rocks, gravel, and roots hurtled through the air in all directions. And the Indians still lived in terror and admiration of such magic. Dynamite. Where had the white man found such thunder-wrecking power? It made many of the Indians restless, unhappy. Some had difficulty adjusting to working for wages. But they liked the white man's guns, to shoot game for food for their families.

Soon Talapus was restless. He told Piele and Cheela he was quitting the crew and going back to Victoria, to talk his friend Waddington into abandoning the project. There were rumors of new outbreaks of smallpox among the Indians at Bella Coola, just to the north, and Talapus thought Waddington should get out before more trouble erupted. He had seen that some white men could be brutal; and he had seen revenge glint in the odd Indian's eye.

"Come back soon, Talapus, I miss you." Cheela called to him as Talapus's feet, on the move again, bore him away and out of sight.

Cheela was frightened now, too, and remembered old Miska's mother's words, "More powerful even than Raven." She was saddened to see her brother going away this time. When Talapus reached Victoria, he approached Waddington, warning him of trouble if he persisted in his undertaking. Talapus the Wolf had nosed many bad odors along the way during his travels; he had watched how the white leaders had behaved and he had heard the mighty Homathko wind — and he feared for his friend and his wagon road to *saghalie illahie,* his road to heaven.

"I travel," Talapus stated. "Like the wolf, I travel and hunt, and I look, and I pick up scents I do not like.

There is discontent and trouble brewing. You are my friend, and I tell you, get out of Homathko."

But Waddington did not listen, and could not understand. He was, as the Homathko and Chilcotin people said, *kahkwe pelton,* crazy like a fool. He ignored the advice as he'd ignored the voice of the nagging wind.

And by midsummer, the strip rape of the Homathko valley had reached one of dozens of points where it had to cross the river, some thirty white-man miles from the head of the inlet. This river crossing was known as ferry headquarters, the place where stores were kept in a well-constructed log house.

The white man's work pushed on. And some of the white men pushed some of the Indian workers in the

same way that they treated the trees and the boulders that stood in their way. Some Indians moved on. Others moved in.

And word spread that a white man attached to Waddington's project, a man called Frederick Whymper, told tales as well as drawing and painting pictures. He told a tale that Waddington's men paid many Indians—he said the Chilcotins—with rifles and ammunition but fed them so badly that they fought with their own dogs, the cayota dogs, for scraps of bone, and bacon rind, and tea leaves that the white men threw out.

As the summer progressed and the road grew, so did the dependency of the working Indians on the white bosses. Many of them had become too fond of the white man's "fire water," his alcohol. And some white workers, it was said, were too fond of supplying it. It made them all the more powerful. And as the Indian workers got drunk, the Indian women "got free," free to the white men. And free, too, to more of the white man's diseases.

Piele worked stoically on, watching. Brewster treated him well enough, and he saw little of the abuse others talked about. Piele received pay in goods—pots and pans for Cheela, an ax for chopping wood. Piele wanted the new way to work, to be good for his people.

By October on the white man's calendar, the crew decided to return to the head of the inlet. Autumn leaves were on the ground; snow covered the mountains and was slowly creeping toward them; the howl of the wolves in the night echoed from the hills. The howl of the Homathko wind sweeping down to *Xwemalhkwu,* swift water, bade summer good-bye. It was time to leave the river to the ice, the winds, and the wolves.

Some of the Indian workers and packers went to the white man boss to receive their payment for work. The white man boss told them the money for payment had to come from Victoria. The money had not come. They would have to wait.

The cold wind of the Homathko did not wait. The cold wind of Homathko howled up the valley like an omen, like the voice of old Miska's mother, like the foreboding that chilled the heart of old Miska.

6
Squint Eye's News

It was in the time of bad weather that Piele's friend with the cunning and knowing eyes came to stay with Piele and Cheela. Squint Eye had a weakness for picking up tales at one village and repeating them in the next. Piele knew he could believe some of Squint Eye's stories, but not all. Squint Eye had much to tell Piele and Cheela.

Squint Eye told Piele there had been more smallpox in Bella Coola and at Lake Nanaloon before the season of bad weather. Talapus had said so, but then the plague's sickness seemed far away. And they had been busy trying the new way of life, the white man's way. But this news sent Cheela racing to find little Toko and feel his forehead. The little boy was well, quite well. Still, this news frightened her.

Squint Eye spoke further. In his travels, he had met Chassis the Ugly One, who had worked for a white man near Tatla Lake. Chassis had been paid with a small brass pot, which the white man assured him was gold, pure solid gold, and worth a fortune. The Ugly One tried to barter the pot to a prospector, but soon found out that he had been fooled.

"A cheat! That's what he was," Squint Eye told them, "a *peshack,* a *cultus* 'great or big' cheat."

Then Squint Eye told them the reason for more smallpox. It was the fault of the white man, he said. While at Lake Nanaloon, Squint Eye had heard that white men had stolen infected blankets from the graves of Indians — Indians who had died from smallpox. The blankets buried with the dead had been sold back to unsuspecting natives.

Miska thought of the button and how it had warned her. She heard again the warning her mother had given when the great seabird-island had glided in and out of Bute.

"They have come back and this is their power," Miska said.

Like *kuckwalla,* like the ants, the white men were eating into Miska's land with their explosives and deadly disease.

Cheela shivered, and held Toko tight. She felt so powerless.

Piele listened to Squint Eye, wondering how much to believe. "Maybe you heard it wrong; maybe your ear on the ground fooled you?" Piele asked.

Squint Eye shook his head. His ear didn't make mistakes. His squinting eyes sometimes saw things that were not there, but his ears could hear.

His ears had heard that some white men had threatened to bring the plague back, especially if the Indians did not do their bidding. The story of the stolen grave blankets made the threat believable. So when the white man started to write the Indians' names in their book, the Indians did the white man's bidding.

Piele began talking of something else, as he could see that Cheela's back was tensed and Miska's eyes were watering. Even he felt a shiver of unease. True, Squint Eye spent much of his time wandering here and there, picking up gossip. And true, Squint Eye's mouth, like the Ugly One's, was sometimes too big. Still, after Squint Eye had left, Piele thought, he would investigate the gossip.

But Squint Eye was offended. "You want those white men crawling all over our country, chasing away our game, cutting down our trees?" he asked. Even he was taking on the white man's sense of ownership. "You want them stealing our women, stealing from our graves? You want that? Then you get that."

"I don't like that," Piele said. "But I got to be sure."

Squint Eye left soon after that, leaving with a warning for Piele to be on his guard.

"I will go to the graves," he said. Cheela and Miska looked at Piele in alarm.

Piele quickly consoled them. "I don't believe this story. This would not happen. Waddington is a good man. If this happened, it wouldn't be his fault. His men, maybe. Yes. But not him."

The crews had not returned to work in Homathko when Piele left for an early spring hunting trip into Tatlayoko Lake country. Twenty white-man's miles northeast of Waddington's camp, Piele met the Chilcotin chief Klatsassin, and two fellow chiefs, Tellot and Tapeet. There was terrible news waiting for Piele.

The vast Cariboo and Chilcotin country indeed had become a burial ground, once again, for many more smallpox victims. Both Tellot and Tapeet had seen in their travels graves that had been desecrated and vandalized. No Indian—firm in his beliefs and superstitions of the spirit world and those departed to it—would molest the graves of his own. Such acts had to be that of the white man.

So Squint Eye was right, Piele thought. Klatsassin was a chief, and trustworthy, as were Tellot and Tapeet. They would not speak of something that was not true. Piele should not have doubted Squint Eye.

The three chiefs moved on toward the Razorback Mountains, west of the lake, but Piele needed now to visit the graves of his two sons. He would see for himself if what he had heard was true. Piele hastened through the forest beneath the overhanging limbs of fir, cedar, and spruce, pushing aside dense tangles of the underbrush. He crossed the swamps where skunk cabbages bloomed, passed the new spring green of grass, cranberry, and Labrador tea bushes. Reaching the lakeshore, he followed the deer trail to an open knoll, where he saw what he had come for. He stood at the burial site while anger mounted, burned, and raged through him, like a plague fever, choking and smothering him. Through misted eyes, he surveyed the damage.

The cedar burial boxes had been ripped from their trees and their lids had been torn away. A nearby circle of charred stones and blackened coals of a long dead fire told him the story. The dry splinters torn from the cedar box had ignited the fire, and the fire had boiled a can of water or cooked dinner for a trapper or prospector—perhaps even one of Waddington's men on a fishing trip. Over and across the burial site ran what looked to Piele to be one of the white man's surveyor's line.

Piele looked for the blankets he had wrapped his sons in, but they were gone. The shock of realization and its companion the fire of anger, rising from the false act of betrayal, gnawed at the pit of his stomach. Slowly he rose and turned away, retracing his steps toward the hut on the Homathko River. It was cruel.

After the first pox which had taken his sons — and after the great white man's epidemic of disease in his year of 1862, which he and his family had escaped — after all that, comes *this*. A white man *spreading* his own disease among the native people on purpose. It was too much!

How many other graves had been tampered with? How many more cases of smallpox because of stolen, diseased blankets? How many more deaths? Rage surfaced within Piele. Soon, Piele told himself, he would call on the gods of his spirit world to witness his vengeance. He, Piele, the usually quiet and unaggressive Chilcotin brave one, would bring down the wrath of thunder and the fear of lightning upon these men, these *cultus* dogs! These plunderers of his land and of his beloved sons!

He traveled on, down toward Homathko, anxious to reach home and share his knowledge with Cheela, who would understand and comfort his intolerable misery, soothe the fire in his belly. Together they would make plans. But he would round up Klatsassin and the others, and they would move and act together, and in force, before another moon rose over the mountains of his valley. He would not stop until every white man in Homathko was dead. Such was his rage. Such were his thoughts.

Piele's anger pushed his steps harder, swifter, and more desperately on, until he could see the outline of the hut in the distance. Now his legs moved faster, until he was running. And when he arrived, he saw that the Homathko wind had arrived with him, and that the wind, too, howled in rage and outrage.

7
Cheela and Piele

Cheela saw Piele coming. She hurried out to meet him, for she had something to tell him. Something that would not please him, and something which she might be wiser to keep to herself. She braced herself against the gusting wind.

But long before he'd reached her, she knew there was anger enough in Piele, and trouble enough of some kind. Cheela saw the anger in his stride, in his swinging arms and clenched fists, and in the haste of his approach. Like an enraged animal fending off an attacker, he came. What had happened? Had another informed Piele of what Cheela was too frightened to tell?

She watched his rapid pace with apprehension, and when he drew near, she waited for him to find breath to speak. In quick gasps he told her of the destruction of the graves. And Cheela was relieved because he did not know. For now, she would hold her news; she would have enough to do calming Piele. Her news could wait until the storm went out of him. She would soothe and baby him until he was once again her easygoing, happy Piele. Then she would speak.

But another voice inside of her told her to remain silent forever. Soon he would be back at work on the road, and their lives could continue as before. For now.

Piele was not easily soothed. He refused to go back to work. His anger refused to subside, as the persistent wind refused to stop. He went instead into the forest. Cheela suspected he met with the chiefs Klatsassin and Tellot, and Chassis the Ugly One. What went on among them she did not know. Piele, on his return, would say little. Perhaps Piele's "father," the great chief Klatsassin, had calmed her husband's anger. After several of these meetings, Piele surprised Cheela by announcing he was going back to work for Brewster. The crews were back and determined to defeat the great mountains in that spring of 1864, white man's time.

Cheela was keeping her own secret from Piele. It was safe buried within her. If the old Miska had not gone down the river, plodding off in search of her medicinal herbs, nothing would have happened. But the old Miska had gone, and only little Toko was there, playing in the shallow pools of the river. He was too little to understand why the white man had gone into his mother's hut. No, Piele must never know about this.

Cheela had made the right decision. Work on the wagon road kept Piele occupied. Day by day, the road slowly advanced, following survey lines through endless miles of rock and timber. Piele changed jobs from packer to laborer to be nearer the shack on the Homathko, but as the road lengthened, he found the distance to be inconvenient. In good weather, he took to camping out near the work site. The crew was now bridge building, falling and moving timbers for skids and for spans to straddle a deep, rock-strewn gorge. Piele watched, and Piele studied the white man's habits.

In a week or two, Piele was more congenial, more carefree. Cheela began to feel safe again, the first time since Piele had returned from the graves. "Piele has made his peace," she thought. She had adjusted to Piele's little "powwows" in the forest with his friends. Men's stuff. But Cheela was young, and naive. Cheela did not know of the weakness and cruelty of human nature, or of the pitfalls that lie waiting for those who walk a narrow rope. Cheela's sense of security was not to last.

Now Chassis the Ugly One was working at a road clearing under the foreman named Biggs. Biggs had sent Chassis for a pail of drinking water from a nearby creek to give to the road clearing crew. Chassis took his time down at the creek. First, he took a long drink himself. Then he wandered along the edge of the creek looking for coon, mink, or otter tracks. Finally, he began sloshing water around in the bucket, emptying it several times to clean the pail before he filled it for the men. When he finally climbed up from the creek, spilling more water as he moved, he arrived with only half a pail of water. Biggs met him with an angry growl and a torrent of abuse and sent him back for another bucket of water.

Chassis resented this. That was the way of Biggs. But Chassis resented it. He would get even with the fat man Biggs. For two small grouse he would hack him up with an axe or a hatchet right then and there. He'd bash his head and chop out his blabbering tongue. Biggs had it coming, for the fat Biggs often abused his workers that way. But if Chassis did exact revenge, he would be in more trouble than he wanted to be bothered with. It would spoil the "softer life" he had sampled with the white man. No. He'd get him some other way. Some way that would loosen his joints but leave him alive to writhe in his pain.

Chassis thought about this for the rest of the afternoon. Anger gnawed at his brain, as hunger gnawed at his stomach. The "softer life" wasn't all good. Many Indian workers were often hungry these days, and sometimes they did indeed fight the dogs for white scraps. Chassis thought about this. The white man had so taken over this part of the Indians' world that the Indian men were not hunting as they had always hunted. Even the plentiful game had fled the white man's influence.

By quitting time, Chassis knew what he would do. Inwardly gloating, his eyes gleaming with malice, his large slash of a mouth more crooked than usual, Chassis drew Piele aside at the end of the day. There was something he had to tell him.

As Chassis spoke, Piele's face froze. Chassis had seen with his own eyes the foreman Biggs with the fat belly, the loud mouth, the foul breath, and the smelly hair, coming away from Piele's hut. This was the time Piele had been at the graves.

"What did he want?"

Chassis shrugged his shoulders. "How should I know?"

"Why would he go there?"

Chassis the Ugly One stared at Piele, his hawkish eyes leering suggestively. "Your wife, Cheela, was she not there?"

Piele did not answer. Perhaps the Ugly One was making trouble, gossiping like an old woman, like old Squint Eye. If it were true, Cheela had told him nothing. It did not make sense. Piele was not going to let

Chassis the Ugly One make a fool of him. Piele asked a few more questions before telling Chassis to keep his tongue silent.

The sun was disappearing behind the mountains as Piele returned home. Streamers of gold and ribbons of crimson crossed the clear evening sky, but Piele did not notice the colors. His mind was in a turmoil. All he ever heard these days, it seemed, was gossip, gossip, gossip, from mouthy people. First Squint Eye, and now Chassis. But Squint Eye had been right, and deep down, Piele knew, no matter how much he tried to deny it, that Chassis was also telling the truth.

Piele had heard of white men bedding down with Indian women any chance they got. And he *had* seen Indian women sharing the tents of some of the road crew. Now he must believe it. He had been too much away. And Biggs had had ample time to take advantage of Piele's absence when he had been at Tatlayoko Lake. Again, red hot anger flamed through him. Grievance after grievance came tumbling to mind. They were not content, these people, with stealing Indian land, infecting them with disease, or wrecking their graves; now they took the Indian women as well. Well, that fit in with the stories of gold miners shooting Indians and some of Waddington's own foremen mistreating their workers. Piele had not been mistreated. But Piele was a good worker; and he was big and strong. Still, Waddington, the white tyee of the road to the sky, was not there to stop any abuse. Strange, these white "chiefs," leading from afar.

Piele said little to Cheela that evening, but he sat watching her furtively as she prepared food for him. After he ate, he waited, this time for little Toko to go to bed. Miska was still visiting at Bute Inlet, following the traditional oolachan run, and he could talk freely

with Cheela, although what he was going to say to her he did not know. Words did not seem to matter anymore. Nothing much did. His world was shattered — the Indians' world was shattered. And they had done nothing. Time for action.

Anyway, Piele's plans were made, as were Klatsassin's, Tellot's, and those others who had joined the secret meetings in the forest. It was just a matter of time now.

Piele watched Cheela silently for several seconds. If Chassis spoke the truth, he wondered, why had Cheela not told him?

"Why do you stare?" she finally asked, a tremor of panic in her voice. Piele had been acting strange all evening.

"Chassis tells me," Piele began, "the job boss, the man called Biggs, came here. Came while I was away."

"Yes, he came."

"Alone?"

She nodded. "I do not know who told him you were away. He came here looking for you, he said. But you were not home — as he saw by looking — so he came in. I was weaving a basket for Miska to take berry gathering. He brought me a gift — he gave me beads, colored beads with bright colors, blue, yellow, red. I sewed them to Toko's moccasins. They are pretty. See what I've made of them."

"Never mind all that!" Piele shouted. "Tell me what he wanted. He does not come here to bring you beads for nothing."

Cheela looked away, unable to meet Piele's stare.

"What did he want?"

"To give me beads."

"Is that all?"

Again Cheela turned away.

"Then it is true. You don't look at me, and what Chassis tells me is true."

Now Cheela faced him. "It is true." Her soft voice pleaded with Piele. "But it is not my fault, Piele. I hit him, I pushed him away, but he was too strong..."

Piele was moving again, away from Cheela.

"Where are you going? Don't leave me. Don't go away again, Piele!"

Piele stormed out into the forest, little knowing or caring where he was going, knowing only that his protective love had been invaded, that his just anger would not be laid to rest so easily. Not this time. He left the hut, and the wind rattled the door that Piele had left swinging.

8
The Massacre

The massacre, when it came, was swift, brutal, and violent.

Piele stormed through the forest mentally banging drums to call Klatsassin and the others onto the warpath. They had held their meetings, held their councils. They had counseled themselves to be patient, in the Indian way, to try to work with the white man, wait for the white man's law to "punish" the bad white men, in the white man's way. But that was not happening. Only more white men were coming, and more bad was happening to Piele's people. Now his anguished brain counseled that they had waited long enough. They had to act before another white man's plague, another white man's lust, another white man's curse fell upon them. Before more Indian men went foolish on the white man's drink.

Piele would speak up.

Klatsassin heard Piele's grievances — as he'd listened to many Chilcotin complaints. Now, he, too, had heard enough.

The great chief sent word to his warriors, among them Tellot, Tapeet, Chassis the Ugly One, and another Chilcotin by the name of Chaddiki. They met together in "war council."

"Is it not enough they bring us the smallpox so that our people die from it as salmon die by the hundreds along our rivers, so that graves cover our land from one end to the other?" Klatsassin thundered. "But each day, new grief."

"They smashed the graves of my two sons, the boys I buried myself," Piele cried. "And then a white man comes to my hut looking for my Cheela. He dares only when I am away. Like a slinking fox he comes. To my hut. *To my hut!* His heart, I'll tear it out and feed it to the coyotes."

"Yes, they take our women," Tapeet said. "It is shame. To white man's eyes, Indian woman is to use and to leave — only 'savages,' not worthy of white man's respect."

"The white man is powerful," Klatsassin declared. "He has guns and gunpowder and trinkets, and he has taken control with all of these things. He has made his own rules and tells us his laws are our laws, and we must follow his laws and suffer his decisions of right and wrong. We have our own code in this matter and we have lived well by it. But our culture, our customs, our codes, our honor, our dead are nothing to them."

These were the thoughts, expressed as we would express them today.

"They are crafty like the fox, and dangerous like the wolverine," Tellot cried. "But we know the ways of foxes and wolverines. Our sinews are stronger, our aim more deadly, our eyes are clearer, our leap quicker. Those who live like foxes will die like foxes, their flesh and innards torn to shreds by the teeth of their own kind. The white man's evil against us calls for revenge."

"We must feed them to the coyotes before their plagues kill us," Klatsassin said. "How else can we save ourselves, our women and our children, and our honor? We must fight them."

"Yes," the men agreed. "The white man eats well but many of us go hungry. White man makes many promises but Indian workers do not get their pay. Yes. We must fight."

It was true. For when the Chilcotins who had not received their pay at the coming of the bad weather in the last working season had gone to Brewster at the beginning of this, they were told the same thing. The pay must come from Victoria, and it had not arrived. There was trouble between the parties, much shouting and, sometimes, shoving.

The Chilcotins had their own guns and bullets with which to fight the fight the chiefs now threatened. They had earned them in their work on Waddington's road and in trade. Yes, the white man had paid the Indians with weapons — and ammunition. To hunt.

"We are ready," Tapeet said solemnly, thrusting his rifle in the air with upstretched arm.

Geese flew overhead, returning to their home in the north, carried on the current of the ever-present wind, the Homathko wind, which breathed heavily through the cedar boughs.

Darkness was falling as the men talked war. Suddenly a new sound came to the Chilcotins' ears. It was three of their fellows coming to join them. The men were agitated, their eyes like moons in excitement. They told a chilling story that fateful night — April 29, 1864, on the white man's calendar.

The man in charge at the ferry landing was cooking his supper over an open fire when they'd arrived, very hungry, very tired, the Chilcotins told Klatsassin. The

fire served three purposes. It cooked Tim Smith's food, gave him light, and when Tim Smith stood in the smoke of the fire, it enabled him to escape the clouds of mosquitoes that were tormenting him. He was confident. Too confident.

The Indians told Klatsassin, Piele, and the others that they had asked Smith for some food but that Smith had sworn at them and cursed them and called them lazy heathens. The younger of the Indians, weary from the smallpox epidemic and his long, lean days and nights of the winter, broke under the insults. He'd raised his rifle and Tim Smith slumped to the ground beside the fire, dead.

That was enough. Words became action. The whole party of enraged men went to the ferry landing. Smith lay where he'd fallen.

The little band of Indians cut the ferry loose, and they plundered the cache of food; many of their people now needed that food, having made themselves dependent on the white man. Then they slipped back up the valley, arriving at the first road crew work camp as early streaks of dawn were cast down the mountainsides into the darkened valleys. The road crewmen slept peacefully in their tents.

Here, the stifled grievances, anger, torment, and fury of the Indians were unleashed. They pulled up the tent pegs and cut the tent guy lines; the canvas collapsed, waking the crew of sixteen. The angry, insulted Chilcotins shot, stabbed, and clubbed again and again through the cloth, until all struggle ceased. Certain that all were dead, the Indians raced north.

The morning of April 30 dawned clear and fresh. At the second camp, a crew of four under Brewster's command were blazing the trail ahead of the road builders. They had risen before dawn, eaten breakfast, and were about to start work when Brewster and his men were fired upon. Brewster and two of the men dropped to the ground and were left where they fell. The fourth man was badly wounded and tried to escape by running to the river. The bullets of the Chilcotins overtook him near the bank, and the current of the river carried his body downstream.

Homathko was awakening from its long winter sleep on that last day of April; the cold thawed from its heart, and its pulse quickened with new life; and there was not a sound on the Homathko trail. No axes swinging, no hammers pounding, no timbers falling. Only a crimson sky at sunset to reflect the blood and carnage on the ground. Tools lay scattered across the clearing, never to be used again on Waddington's road. Even Indian girls' footwear was found at the first camp of carnage. And the Homathko wind droned down the valley.

The avengers vanished into the hills and the forests. They were joined by others along the way.

Someone killed a settler at Puntzi Lake. Still, the "hostiles," as they were becoming known, moved on.

Soon the group crossed the path of a man named McDonald, who was bringing down supplies on forty-two packhorses to the mines at Fort Alexandria on the Fraser River. His party of eight was attacked at Nancoutloon Lake, seventy-five miles east of Bentinck Arm and Bella Coola. They fled to the brush and defended themselves by making fortifications of earth. When they left their shelter three days later, they were ambushed on the trail. McDonald's horse was shot from beneath him; McDonald mounted another horse, which was also shot down. The horses ran between the packers and the Indians, confused and frightened by the sound of the firing guns. While five of the packers escaped, McDonald and two others were killed.

After this, Klatsassin moved toward upper Tatla Lake country with Tellot and Tapeet. Chassis and Chaddiki and the others also hid in the mountains. Piele hid, too, for a time. But he made a swift visit to the hut on the Homathko to see Cheela, who met him later in the forest, at night, with food. These stolen moments together were short, for Piele dared not stay long near his hut and family. Then, as the heat of the chase cooled and the danger of capture lessened, Piele returned to Homathko once again. He told Cheela only that he, Piele, the Indian brave, had done what he'd had to do.

But the white authorities governing the vast mainland colony of British Columbia from New Westminster saw the attack in a much different light. News of the massacre outraged and shocked the public. News that had come from bruised, bleeding,

and battle-weary survivors of the massacre. News from an Irishman named Buckley, who had been stabbed in the initial attack, had snuck free after the Indians had left, and had gone upstream to warn Brewster. Buckley had found three bodies, one of them a mutilated Brewster. News came from a Dane named Petersen,

who had jumped from his blankets when he was wakened by the attack and was struck at by an ax-wielding Indian. Petersen ducked aside but was shot in the arm. He staggered to the river, whose swift and turbulent water tumbled him over the rocks. News came from a man called Mosley, who also said he had escaped — because a tent pole had crashed down on his head. He had later managed to hide along the riverbank till all was quiet.

The three met by fate at the ferry landing, where Smith's body lay. They carried the news.

The authorities declared immediate action must be taken. These wild, murderous savages must be caught and shown that the young colony of British Columbia would not countenance such rebellion. For rebellion it was seen to be. Reports said hordes of Indians were gathering as insurgents. White people fled the territory. Outraged citizens called for swift and violent retribution.

The hunt was on. And for Cheela and Toko and the old Miska, who lived alone on the Homathko, the long wait had begun. And the wind sighed.

9
The Hunt

Governor Frederick Seymour, a newcomer to the colony, lost no time in organizing a group to bring in the murderers. A party of thirty-eight volunteers under the command of Chief Inspector of Police Chartres Brew left on the H.M.S. *Forward,* traveling up the coast from New Westminster to Bute Inlet. Brew's party was to make its way into Chilcotin country by traveling along the Bute Inlet route and then inland along the Waddington trail. A second party of sixty-five men was rounded up in the Cariboo under the command of Gold Commissioner William G. Cox. They were to travel through the Interior from Fort Alexandria and meet up with Brew at Puntzi Lake near the Chilcotin River.

But there were delays for both parties. The first to encounter trouble was the Cox party. The steamer *Enterprise,* which operated from Quesnel on the Fraser River, broke down. The men built rafts to reach Fort Alexandria. From there, Cox led his men westward to Puntzi Lake.

The Indians, at first, were alarmed but had heard the group coming, and prepared to attack. Cox hurriedly built a log fort and set up his hunting headquarters behind its walls. He sent out a scouting party, but it was attacked and they retreated to the safety of the fort. As a precaution against further attacks, Cox flew a white flag on top of the fort, signaling friendship, and tried to think out a plan.

Meanwhile, after leaving Bute Inlet, Brew's party realized the precipitous rock walls of the river canyon and the dense timbered terrain of the mountainous country were formidable and dangerous barriers. After a hazardous journey up the Homathko River, they reached the ferry crossing, finding only the body of Tim Smith and the looted food cache. After burying Smith, they traveled upriver and found the other victims of the massacre, lying where they had fallen.

Beyond this point, the country was so rough and the obstacles so great that Brew and his men were forced to turn back. It was impossible to find their way into Indian country from Bute Inlet, as the horses could not make it through the mountains or passed the swift-running river.

While Brew fought his way up Waddington's route, Governor Seymour was hosting the Fraser Valley Indians on the Queen's birthday. About 3,500 Indians came to the party, pitching a huge tent city on the town's outskirts. It was a very successful party.

Brew, turned back by the terrain at Bute, traveled back to New Westminster to seek advice from Governor Seymour. They decided to try the Palmer trail, built two years earlier in 1862, which ran from Bella Coola inland to Fort Alexandria. Seymour accompanied this party.

On July 7, nearly two months after the party had first set out, Brew arrived at Cox's fort. The governor was angry that Cox was "hiding" in his fort and ordered everybody to get out and hunt down the culprits. Then Brew struck out with his twenty-eight volunteers toward Chilco Lake and into the mountains where Klatsassin was said to have gone. The men found nothing more than dead ashes of recent campfires. They found no evidence they could recognize to determine whether the Indians had departed into the hills, the mountains, or the forest.

The white men were outmaneuvered, outdistanced, and outsmarted by those whom they chased. The Indians knew every inch of their country. They knew how to elude their pursuers. While Brew was a persistent and determined officer, and his men, his volunteers, were disciplined and had been carefully selected, they did not know the land or the craft of stalking, as the Indians did. However, Brew did succeed in keeping the Indians on the move, allowing them little time to hunt and fish for food.

It is written that the governor sent word to the powerful Indian leader, Delitus Anahiem of the Chilcotins, asking him not to support the renegades. Anahiem agreed.

One of Cox's men was Donald McLean, the former Hudson's Bay Company chief at Fort Kamloops. He was eager to capture the fleeing Indians. In the middle of July, he took an Indian guide to scout the area, which he knew quite well. So well did he know the country and the Indians that he seemed to consider his life charmed. His guide heard the click of a gun and warned McLean. McLean contemptuously ignored the warning. The next moment, he lay dead on the ground, a bullet through his heart. The guide crawled back to the post. The renegade Indians scampered stealthily farther into the deep cover of the forest. It has been written that Klatsassin was among them.

Another month of hunting passed, another month of Homathko wind; then the search was called off. Cox and Brew were tired, discouraged, and beaten. The shortage of provisions, plus the enormous daily costs of the expedition, brought the chase to a close. Brew's party moved on to Bella Coola, and back to New Westminster.

Klatsassin, Piele, and the others had kept an eye on Cox and the movements around the fort. Some Chilcotins had even ventured in to trade with Cox's men. Cox himself stayed behind the walls most of the time — away from the Chilcotins, away from the Homathko wind — so he wasn't much of a threat. Klatsassin saw that the tyee of white tyees, Governor Seymour, had gone with the party to Bella Coola; he had not seen him come back.

With the stalking over, Piele returned to his hut on the Homathko and made plans with Cheela to return to Tatlayoko Lake. Piele was at peace now. He had helped rid his land of two plagues: the white man and the smallpox.

Waiting to return to civilization, Cox was annoyed at the failure of himself and his men to capture even one Indian.

Klatsassin, meanwhile, was also getting restless. He, too, wanted to return to his home and family. The white man had failed to capture them in the wilds, with the advantages of guns, ammunition, and food. Before, Klatsassin thought it unlikely they could return to their homes in safety. But now the chief was doubtful of the white man's ability to hunt at all.

Klatsassin and the others were ready to return to living as they always had: hunting, fishing, and wandering. Summer was slipping away and they were weary of the chase. Soon the cooler nights of autumn would be upon them, and then the snow would fall. Was the white man not having similar thoughts? Klatsassin wondered. When the snow lay deep in the mountain passes and valleys, food or supplies couldn't get through from Quesnel or Fort Alexandria. Cox and his men would starve. And, besides, they had made it abundantly clear they knew little about survival in the wilderness. They could not catch an Indian, let alone catch a fish or a moose to eat. They would quickly perish, Klatsassin decided.

There was no reason that everyone could not return home, the chief thought. Surely Cox was tired of the foreign way of living. Perhaps there could be an agreement made. After all, the man had been flying a white flag atop his fort since his arrival at Puntzi Lake. He was still offering his friendship. In fact, he, or as some say, Governor Seymour, had sent an emissary of peace to the Chilcotin leader Alexis. Alexis, too, was said to be preparing for war, but the emissary calmed his fears about the white man's intentions. Alexis agreed to act as intermediary and to offer the rebel Indians amnesty for surrender.

So Klatsassin sent one of his men to Cox with a message: What are you prepared to offer in return for our surrender? It was worth a try. Cox replied by loading the man with a sack of flour, tobacco, and other gifts. His message to Klatsassin was that he would be glad to see them, that he would not hurt them in his camp, but would turn them over to the "big chief." But he also warned if they did not come, he would hunt them down and kill each and every one of them, and he would keep on their trail until the snow came.

Threats coming from the safety of the fort merely made Klatsassin smile. But the offer to meet without being harmed, together with the gifts from Cox, seemed reasonable enough. It meant, Klatsassin said to himself that the gift of tobacco indicated that he, Klatsassin, would smoke the pipe of peace with Chief Seymour. It was agreed for all parties to meet at Fort Chilcotin, an old Hudson's Bay Company fort.

Klatsassin sent out runners to beckon those involved in the massacre to come to the meeting. This false sense of security, whether intentional or not on Cox's part, was the trap that Klatsassin walked into.

The group arrived at the fort, where Klatsassin spoke: he had brought in seven men involved in the massacre, as well as himself; he was returning one horse, one mule, and twenty dollars to the government as a token of his good faith. He introduced himself as Klatsassin, and those with him as Tellot, Tapeet, Piele, Chassis, Chaddiki, Cheloot, and Sanstaki. There are more, he told the white men, but it would not be possible to find them before early spring, when they came to the lake to fish and hunt. Three of his own braves had been killed, he explained, and one of those by McDonald.

Suddenly, Klatsassin and his men were surrounded by armed men who informed them they were prisoners. They were told to lay down their arms. Confused, they did so, except for Tellot, who grabbed his rifle by the muzzle and smashed it against a tree. Then he threw his knife to the ground, shouting, that the queen's men were great liars.

10
Reflections

The white lawmakers would never catch Piele or Klatsassin, Cheela was sure. In time the hunters would go away and the hunted could return home. To the hunters, it was early September, and the days were warm and soft, the nights without wind. A cold fog clung to the early dawn. The chill was a warning to Cheela that wood and bark and dry sticks were needed for their fires before winter. Homathko was a cold, hard country when the glacial winds came down from the mountains.

Cheela looked to the mountain of *Xwe7xw*. This mountain was once a man that used to wander frequently. Cheela, thinking of this, was reminded of Piele and Talapus, the two men she loved most in her life. The individual peaks along the southwest side of Bute Inlet are said to be the wife, daughter, and dogs of *Xwe7xw*. *Xwe7xw* is a special mountain, she had told Piele, for he is the keeper of the north wind, that infamous Bute Inlet wind, which is the curse of travelers. "It is important never to look at *Xwe7xw* and make fun of him or throw things in his direction. If you do, the north wind will start to blow."

If only the wind would blow now, Cheela thought, to make the white men's travels much too difficult to continue the search. The wind would blow all the white men away and all the Indian men home.

It was more than a moon since she had watched Piele leave with Klatsassin's messenger. She had been alarmed, but Klatsassin was a Chilcotin chief, respected and influential. Piele was safe with him. Hearing no news of them for a long time meant they were still hiding and could be home any day. Just as Talapus the Wolf could return any day.

Cheela had much work still to do in preparation for winter. A dry cache would be needed to store the fish she had caught and would catch and the berries she had pressed into pulp and dried in flat cakes. There were clothes to mend, skins to soften, moccasins to make, cedar bark.thread and strippings to prepare.

Miska used to help with these things, but the old Miska was slower now. Her joints were stiff and her aches and pains were crippling her. She limped about with the aid of a strong, stout Arbutus branch she had found near the mud flats of Bute Inlet.

Miska, after grunting and snorting herself awake, was more cheerful than usual. Miska was going to make the most of this temporary relief from pain, she said to Cheela. She would travel to the bog while it was still mild and fill her basket, the basket Cheela had woven for her, with mountain blueberries and late red elderberries, as well as Labrador tea leaves. Miska limped off into the forest.

These days, Miska's magic syrups were for herself. The liquid eased the soreness in her body. A small portion of boiled dogwood root gave her strength, while cascara bark made a potent, cleansing brew which carried away the crippling poisons in her system.

Cheela measured time by the berries ripening on the bushes. In the season of the flying flocks, Cheela and Miska gathered sweet briar and wild rhubarb, and tender shoots of bracken fern, to be peeled and eaten with dried salmon eggs. They collected the shoots of salmonberry, thimbleberry, and blackcap bushes, and dug the roots of wild violet, wild onion, chocolate lilies, and sword ferns. These they steamed in underground steaming pits. Later in the spring, they harvested Indian celery, or cow parsnip. You had to be careful not to leave the outer skin on the stalks, Miska always reminded Cheela, for your lips will blister and your skin will discolor.

Next came the season of the salmonberry. Wild strawberry, blackcaps, thimbleberries, trailing wild blackberries are abundant in the country of Bute Inlet and Homathko. At the height of summer, the time of the wasps, there were soapberries, huckleberries, and Oregon grape berries.

In late August, on the white man's calendar, there were salal berries and gooseberries. And in September, it was the time of the dog salmon, red elderberries, and mountain blueberries. Miska loved berries garnished with oil or grease: oolachan oil was her favorite. It was rich, and it was preventative against colds, aches, and chest miseries.

The tidal waters of Bute Inlet provided their winter supply. Cheela remembered Cumsack Creek and how she and old Miska had dug clams at low tide. Sometimes by the light of pitchwood torches they had dug in the sand. To make sure there would be a good harvest of clams, they would spit upon the first clam dug on each excursion.

But now the old Miska could not make it easily over the winding trail which led to the inlet, and she depended on Cheela to bring her what she could. It was her pace, Miska said, that was slowing down, not her spirit. When the aged, watery eyes began to burn, or light up from something deep within her, Cheela was aware of the brave, quiet courage and determination with which Miska faced life and death. Cheela loved and pitied the old Miska, and she would do what she could to ease Miska's miseries. In the same way she had loved and pitied her dying sons whom she could not help, she loved and pitied Miska. Tenas Pootie and Keeto had cried as they burned, as they died their slow deaths. And now Miska, who had stopped her crying, was lame and feeble. Cheela would suffer with Miska until she joined the spirits in the land of the dead.

Cheela herself had aged little physically. Her face was still round and free of lines and wrinkles, her eyes soft and smiling as when she had first met Piele. And she was strong, strong enough to do the extra work, which helped pass the time until Piele came home.

Three moons ago one of Brew's men had come to the hut, asking where Piele and the others were hiding. Cheela had pointed in the opposite direction from where she knew Piele to be, for he had snuck home for a few precious moments, a few precious nights. Piele had told her how they had camped right under the noses of the white men, how they could hear their voices speaking with their two tongues. Piele and Klatsassin and the others had quietly moved away, leaving behind a smoldering campfire for their pursuers to find. It was easy.

Soon the white men would have to give up their search, Cheela was sure. Soon Piele would be home. On the Homathko wind, Piele would be home.

11
The Trial

Under armed guard, Commissioner Cox had swiftly transferred the prisoners to Fort Alexandria, then to Quesnel via the steamer *Enterprise*. The white authorities believed the prisoners should be tried immediately, thereby lessening the risk of escape and also serving as a warning to other Indians not to plot similar rebellions.

At Quesnel, a dirty log cabin served as a makeshift jail, a partition at one end of the cabin forming a cell. The heat from the pot-bellied stove did not reach the other end of the cabin, where eight Indians crouched in the dark. Here the Chilcotins were shackled to the walls for over a month, awaiting the arrival of the judge. Waiting and remembering.

Judge Matthew Baillie Begbie arrived in Quesnel on September 27, 1864, and the trial began the following day. Judge Begbie carefully recorded the evidence in longhand.

A lawyer whose interest lay in the Bentinck Arm route, from Bella Coola to the goldfields in the Cariboo, acted in defence of the accused. A French Canadian named Baptiste and a man from Cox's expedition were appointed by the court to interpret the words of the Chilcotin people. The stage was set.

Commissioner Cox was sworn in and repeated the story of Klatsassin and his men arriving at the fort with a horse, a mule, and the twenty dollars as peace offerings. Cox said he had promised not to hurt the Indians in his camp and that he would hand them over to the "big chief." By the big chief, he said, he meant Judge Begbie, who would try them, not Seymour, who would talk with them.

Then the accused were brought into the courtroom one at a time. (Sanstaki and Cheloot were not brought to trial, even though Klatsassin had named them as part of the uprising. No witnesses could testify against Chaddiki, so he too was acquitted.)

One of the witnesses appearing in court was Squint Eye. He told the court that he had worked for Brewster and that he had heard about the killing of Tim Smith at the ferry camp. He was not involved himself, but he had heard much. Squint Eye was never short of words or gossip. But he was short of memory at times like this, and that proved to be most convenient — for him.

"This is all hearsay," said the man who spoke on behalf of the accused. "No words of the Indians, other than Klatsassin's, can be taken as evidence." And so Squint Eye stepped down from the stand, a free man.

Tellot was called to the stand and told the jury that he was an old man, too old to do any harm, and that another Indian, Quotsinsty, would have killed him, Tellot, if he had not joined with the men. All he had done was take a small hatchet and throw a couple of blows with it.

When Tapeet came to the stand, he was all innocence. It had never occurred to him, he told the jury, to kill a white man until another Indian, a leader, urged him to do so. It was only as a last resort — and then only to please the leader — that he had taken his gun and shot a man called Manning, the settler who had died at Puntzi Lake, after the massacre. It was the first time he had ever killed anyone, he said. No, Tapeet was just not that kind of man.

Chassis claimed that he had not killed the man at the ferry landing. He had fired one shot at the same time as several other Indians, but he did not know if his shot killed anyone. Chassis the Ugly One, with his misshapen mouth, tried to convey with a twisted smile that he was innocent.

When Piele took the stand, he was still incensed and seething over the way his group had been tricked and captured. He was not going to tell these inquisitors anything. If it had not been for that white man Cox and his white flag and his gifts of tobacco and his empty promises, he would not be here. He would be moving with Cheela and Toko to Tatlayoko, not chained and staked like an animal in a trap awaiting a long, slow death. In a cage, six feet by seven, a wooden coop. With seven others. In a pen with bars over a single window too high to see through. Men who kept other men from being free were *cultus* dogs, and these white men had kept him in the dark, dank smelling enclosure for too many nights.

No, he would tell these cheats nothing. What did they know about that foreman Biggs? About the unfair treatment at the work camps and the nonpayment of their wages. What did they know about Piele's sons and their ravaged graves?

The judge did not appear to ask these questions; the judge did not know the language of the Chilcotin or the Salish, and Piele did not know English. And for the most part, Piele could not understand the interpreter, who seemed to mumble a lot.

The courtroom gave Piele the shivers. He had never seen anything like it, or known such a strange way to determine if a man was guilty or innocent of a crime. Piele only knew his people's way: if the man had committed a crime, he was tracked down and an arrow was slammed through his heart.

Piele was aware that the judge was looking at him and mouthing the strange words he could not comprehend. The judge was dressed in ceremonial clothes, in accordance with some kind of Queen Victoria tribal custom.

"Did you kill anyone during the uprising?" asked the interpreter.

'If I didn't it wasn't for lack of trying,' Piele thought.

Aloud he said, "I don't know." And truthfully he didn't know. So many shots had been fired at random, no one knew for sure whose bullet had struck down man or horse.

"What about McDonald. Did you kill McDonald?"

"No, for sure, not him. I fired but missed and killed his horse instead."

"What happened then?"

"McDonald leaped onto another horse, and someone shot that horse."

"Who?"

"I am not sure."

"And what did McDonald do then?"

"He ran into the brush and started firing from behind a tree."

"Who killed McDonald?"

"I don't know."

"Did you kill anyone at all in the uprising?"

"I do not know."

Piele was led away and taken back to the cell in the cabin, where he again waited and waited and fumed with rage as he crouched in the dark. If he ever got out of this trap he would never be caught again. If there were any way to escape, he would take it. He'd been away from home for too long, away from Homathko. If that man who now sat in the courtroom judging him had endured what he had, suffered the indignities and the injustices that he and his people had, would he not have done the same?

When it was his turn to speak, Klatsassin told the jury he had become angry enough to kill when a white man threatened to bring about a second plague of smallpox, simply by writing their names in a book. Five of the Indians saw the man writing names in his book.

Then Klatsassin said he had smoked the pipe of peace with Cox, and the pipe was filled with tobacco the white man had given him. Cox had promised the Indians would be transferred to the "big chief." This certainly meant Governor Seymour. Instead, here they were, before a man dressed as an eagle or a raven, with hair of white on its head and a black, billowy cloak over its body. This was some other kind of chief in the white man's world taking part in another bizarre ritual. It was like his people's costumes and masks and rituals. But it was not like them. The white judge and he were alike. But they were not alike. Klatsassin did not understand the power this man held. The great Chilcotin leader was bewildered by it all.

The black eagle with the wig on its head asked Klatsassin—the chief of his own people—if he would have entered Cox's camp if he had known the consequences. Did the eagle assume that Klatsassin's men were ready to give up because they had no flour, and could not hunt or fish, or light a fire for fear of detection? Had they not lived since the beginning of time on this land without the help of the white man's flour? The Indians had outfoxed the white man for over three moons, and they would still be free if they had not been foolish enough to trust the words of the white man. They had believed, Klatsassin said, and the trust had been sealed by the smoking of the pipe of peace.

Later Piele and Klatsassin decided that the man Cox had two tongues. Just as the judge had two heads of hair, and two coats, and two standards to live by. One for the white man and one for the Indian.

The evidence had been heard. Klatsassin and Tellot were found guilty of murder by the jury. But they disagreed on whether Piele, Chassis, and Tapeet were guilty of the same crime. Judge Begbie reminded the jury that if five men attack in unison, and any one of the attacked party is killed, then all five men should be held responsible, and each is guilty of murder.

And so Klatsassin, Tellot, Tapeet, Chassis, and Piele were sentenced to be hanged.

Back in their cell, chained to the wall, Piele listened hard. He could hear the Homathko wind.

12
Shadows

Cheela was thinking of winter. She thought of the cold reaching the miners working their claims in the Cariboo and Chilcotin country. The miners searched the hillsides for gold, pawing through the earth and shaking pans in the creeks and rivers in hope of finding even a glint of it, leaving their poison in the water. The white men went wild to get the gold. It was only a soft yellow metal. Why would anyone go through so much trouble to get it? There were many other things to do in life that were far more pleasant, like watching the world in its autumn beauty. All along the Homathko hillsides, maple, cottonwood, and alder leaves were turning brown, red, and gold. Now *this* was the real gold: the golden beauty of a leaf or a tree of golden leaves, or a stalk of fireweed laden with purple blossoms, or the song of birds and their noisy chatter as they stuffed themselves with overripe salal berries that grew alongside the riverbank. All of this was the gold and the beauty of the earth, Cheela thought.

Soon the salmon would swim up the Homathko to spawn. Cheela watched them struggle upstream by the hundreds each year. She loved to watch the Salmon

People. These mysterious people returned each year to see her, to give her food for winter. Piele speared them from the banks and Cheela smoked them over maple or alder wood fires until they were dried and cured hard as a board. Later, the salmon were stacked away in a cache.

After a long, dry summer, Cheela could hear the salmon splashing and flopping about, waiting at the entrance of a stream for rain to swell the river and let them through. Discolored and decaying, the salmon fanned holes with their tails in the bottom of a stream and deposited their eggs. Then, again using their tails, they covered the spawn with silt and sand. With their bodies rapidly decomposing, these mysterious people who lived beneath the sea, died.

Cheela loved this time of year because it was in the season of the Salmon People she and Piele had met. It was the time of year when the sun was still warm with a soft, mellow glow, which warmed Cheela through and through. These were days for watching the thistle down drifting on the air before it settled in a sheltered nook. Cheela always loved these days with Piele.

The sun's warmth was like a lubricant to Miska's aching bones. Her aches left her and she felt young again. Miska sat outside and painstakingly wove cedar lacings into beautiful baskets with her old fingers. Later she would dye them, using alder bark to make red, lichen to make yellow, and hemlock bark for brown. Oregon grape created a yellow green, and copper produced blue green.

Today Miska talked much to Cheela and Toko. Her talk lately was only of Piele, and of the past: Piele, when he was small like Toko, bringing her lilies, blue and yellow violets, and tiny blue stardrops that grew on the banks of the creek; Piele, a young boy, making his first bow and arrow. She also remembered Piele being chased by a grizzly bear after stumbling upon her cubs. Piele had run until he fell gasping into the hut. Miska had blamed herself for this. She should have been watching the boy, seeing that he didn't wander too far from home. Like his father. She had been preoccupied at the time, couldn't remember now, after all these years, what she had been doing to forget Piele. After that, she watched him more closely. Then Piele had left Bute Inlet to learn how to be a hunter, to be a man, under Klatsassin's tutelage.

Now, again, Piele had wandered away, and Miska did not know where he was. It was this not knowing that kept her mind on Piele.

Cheela also thought of nothing else. Throughout the day she glanced toward the distant hills, her eyes always seeing *Xwe7xw,* even though she was careful not to look upon him directly. The air was soft and balsam-sweet, and the sun warm, and Cheela longed for Piele. She dreamed of the things they would do when he returned, the words they would speak, the places they would go, the love they would share. Cheela ached with loneliness for Piele, remembering his laughter, his courage, and his love. She gathered Toko in her arms and held him close. Every day Toko was growing with the daylight and Piele was not here to see it.

The warm, quiet days passed. Cheela watched the shadows gather as the sun faded and the cool night entered, chilling their shelter. The cold, along with the shadows, brought new fears and more questions. Where was Piele tonight? And Klatsassin and Chassis the Ugly One? Did they sleep, or were they, like herself and Miska, half awake, half listening, then suddenly alert as the night deepened? They heard sounds. Perhaps it was Piele returning. The hunted and the hunters were close by. Miska was also awake, listening and nervous. Miska's thoughts returned, like salmon to their place of birth, to the memory that none were safe in this land anymore, not since the boat had anchored offshore at Bute Inlet many years ago.

She spoke to Cheela: *"Nika tumtum Kahkwa cole illahie,* my heart is like winter."

And winter comes too soon, thought Cheela. And we are still here by this cold, cold river.

"Kah nesika Klatawa, where should we go?" Miska spoke, as if reading Cheela's mind. Cheela could not answer. She did not know where they would go or what they would do if Piele did not come soon. She soothed Miska back to sleep. Then Toko awakened from a bad dream. Cheela went to him and soothed him back to his pleasant dreams. When he was quiet, she stood gazing out of the doorway. It was a clear night with a moon that shone on the land before her.

Cheela stiffened. Every muscle in her body tensed. Something outside moved, then vanished into the shadows. Whether it was a man or an animal, Cheela did not know. Perhaps another sweaty, smelly, evil Biggs, wanting an Indian woman whose man was far away. Perhaps Biggs was not dead after all. Perhaps he would return.

But this time Cheela would be ready. Piele had given her a gun, one he had traded with a white man for a cedar canoe. He had shown her how to use it. This time, Cheela would shoot, and she would make sure the white man was dead. There would be a bullet waiting for the white *mamooks* who bothered her again. Cheela quietly loaded the gun and waited.

An owl hooted from somewhere in the forest. Other muffled noises of the night sounded, but Cheela saw no movement. Inside the hut, Miska was snoring hoarse, rattling snores that threatened to waken her at any moment. Toko slept, his bad dream forgotten.

As the pale gray light of morning grew, the Homathko wind eased — Cheela's fear eased. Her tensed muscles relaxed and her courage returned. The sun would soon be up and it would be warm. On such a day, surely only good would follow, Cheela thought.

Surely today Piele would come. Surely the faithful wind would bring him home.

13

The Execution

The last hope for reprieve for Klatsassin and Piele and the others rested with Governor Seymour. He was the man who had the power to grant clemency.

Judge Begbie wrote to him explaining the weaknesses of the court's case.

The prisoners had not been hunted down and brought in, he wrote; they had come to Cox's camp voluntarily, believing it safe to do so. In the Indian mind, the exchange of gifts and the smoking of the pipe of peace represented a sacred trust in a man's word. Cox had promised that no harm would come to them in Cox's camp.

While Begbie had no doubt these men were guilty of murder, these points were flaws in the trial's case. Had Cox spoken with a "forked tongue," as Klatsassin claimed? Besides that, the judge pointed out, the white man had come and used the Indians' land.

Governor Seymour studied the Judge's concerns. In the end, he decided, the case for the Crown versus murder took precedence over surrender versus murder. Seymour, therefore, refused to intercede and Judge Begbie's decision stood.

On October 2, 1864, Piele, Klatsassin, Tellot, Tapeet, and Chassis the Ugly One were to die. They were to hang from a noose until it was over.

Breakfast was meager. Food was expensive, so a prisoner's portion was carefully measured out. (Not that it mattered to the men. A condemned man has little thought for food or drink.) Following the meal, the five were led to the scaffold, which had been readied the day before. A crowd of curious onlookers had gathered, and were milling about. Waiting.

There was Klatsassin, standing tall and straight, prepared to meet his end with the courage and dignity that befitted an Indian chief. When a compassionate soul offered him a drink, Klatsassin refused. He, Klatsassin, the Chilcotin chief, was proud and would meet death as a brave Indian.

There was Tapeet, leaving no one doubting his strength and courage as he spoke to his friends and fellow "freedom fighters," telling them to have courage. He told several Carrier Indians witnessing the scene to quit fighting the white man, as it would only get them to see the Great Father.

There was Chassis the Ugly One, handicapped from birth with too large a mouth. Perhaps it had been easy for Chassis to kill under the circumstances, but it was doubtful it was easy for Chassis to die, or to understand why he had to.

There was Tellot, who was wise enough to have eluded his pursuers indefinitely. But something had gone wrong. "What does it matter?" he thought. "I am an old man now." Still, if he only had that hatchet here with him, he would chop anyone's hand who tried to stop him from running.

There was Piele, the youngest of them all, friend and son to Klatsassin. It was too late to escape and he knew it. His mind churned a hundred anguished and chaotic thoughts. But he had reviewed his grievances and justified his actions. His sons, Tenas Pootie and Keeto, had died from the white man's disease; their graves had been plundered and the blankets stolen by the white man, and finally, Cheela had been taken by the revolting Biggs. That dirty *cultus* dog! He would not trouble Cheela or any Indian woman again. The coyotes would have found him by now and torn his heart out. The coyotes would have squabbled and fought over his stinking carcass. Teeth bared and mouths slobbering, they would have ripped Biggs to pieces and crunched his bones to meal. No, that man Biggs would never touch another Indian woman.

It was October, the season of the falling leaf, the time that he and Cheela loved. But who would care for his Cheela now? And who would teach Toko how to hunt and fish or make a bow and arrow? Who would show him how to skin a deer, track a moose or a bear or a wolf, make axes and hammers from stone, or carve a canoe out of cedar? Piele wanted to be the one to explain how to heat the rocks and pour water over them, how to place the dugout over the steam so the wood would soften with the heat, how to stretch and shape the canoe using poles placed inside of it. How you leave the poles there until the wood cools. Who would bring up Toko to be a fine and proud Indian?

If only he could be on the banks of the Homathko now, spearing fish for Cheela to smoke. He would hunt *mowitch* and moose for their winter cache. He would travel with his family to Tatlayoko where the game fattened in the lush swamps and meadows. And soon Toko would be old enough to go along on the hunt.

It had been too many moons now since he had hidden outside the hut and Cheela had brought him

food, and they had made love beneath the trees, beneath the stars and the moon and the sweet-scented cottonwood. If only there were some way he could send word to Cheela, who waited for him on the banks of the Homathko. But there was nothing he could do.

Nothing. He could not say good-bye to his mother, to his son, or to his woman. This was a new–and frightening–experience.

If only this were a bad dream, a vision, like his uncle Chikatt was famous for. He and Klatsassin and the others would not really die, as the man in the wig and black flapping cloak had said they would. If only he could escape. Run like Talapus the Wolf. Talapus. He was out there. Free.

But it was too late. Too late. They had been led out. One by one. To the end of their time on earth.

They were blindfolded, and a missionary offered a prayer "for the souls of those about to depart." Tapeet offered final words of courage to his fellow braves when there was silence.

The signal was given and the drops fell. An awed silence fell over the crowd, who saw five bodies hanging at the end of five ropes: choking, squirming, swinging, then motionless. The hearts could no longer pump blood through strangled veins, and the bodies, like the pendulums of unwound clocks, ceased to sway.

The curious, morbid crowd began moving again, and the five Chilcotins were cut down and carted away for burial in the woods near Quesnel, not far from the Cariboo Road. They were buried in the ground, in the manner of the white man, and a crude wooden cross was planted to mark the graves. The forest sheltered them, and the silence mourned them. Wings of the eagles flew overhead, the wild geese called, the golden leaves of autumn fell, and the snows of winter covered them in silence. The mighty Homathko wind, the wind from *Xwe7xw,* stood still for a time.

And the years forgot them.

14

Cheela

Perhaps today Piele will come! This was the thought Cheela wakened to each day.

She told Miska, "He'll be home before the salmon spawn." The salmon had spawned, but no Piele. She told Miska, "He'll be home before the leaves fall." The leaves had fallen, but no Piele. Then finally, "He'll be home before the bear sleeps."

Miska shook her head. She had lived too long, seen too much to share Cheela's hope.

As the days passed, Cheela began to doubt her own words of consolation. She worried most in the evenings, and part of the long, dark nights. Toko was asleep and Miska sat sipping her brew of wild herb leaves, and all was quiet.

When there was no other sound in the hut but the thrust and pull of her bone needle, Cheela was afraid. She sewed through the soft seal leather, making warmers for Toko's hands when he played outside. She also made warmers for the old Miska, whose blood was thin with age, and whose bony fingers had stiffened again with the early winter wind and could no longer pull the thread through the hide.

Though Piele had said no harm could come to them now that the white men were dead, Cheela was not so sure. She thought of the moving shadow she had seen half a moon ago. She wondered if more white men had come to replace those killed. In faraway places, such as New Westminster and the Cariboo and Lillooet countries, there were governments and men who made laws, and these men were more powerful even than the biggest Indian chief. How safe could Piele be? How safe could any of them be?

Stars glittered above the mountains and treetops in the black night sky. It was passing the time when the north wind brought colors of gold and scarlet to the hillsides and scattered sparkling frost across the land.

This was also a time of warning, a vision of what lay ahead in the coming months. She knew too well the risks and dangers a winter camped in Homathko could mean. Without Piele home, Cheela would have to prepare for the winter alone. There would be wood to bring in, much more than she had now. It would have to be piled inside the shelter, for when blizzards blew down upon them from the Homathko ice fields, it would not be safe to put her head out the door. The storms would blow from the icebound, towering peaks, from the coldest and bleakest mountains of the Homathko ice fields, and of course from *Xwe7xw*. There would be no traveling at all when these winds blew. There would be only survival.

As a child, Cheela had watched the gales from the storms blow great spumes of salt spray across the inlet, spray which fell back to the water in frozen crystals of ice. Here, the wind would cut across them on the edge of the Homathko River, a bitter, biting wind, that would lash them with cold. It would be a struggle to keep Miska and Toko warm.

She had heard the Bute Inlet wind whistling and howling down the canyon walls of the Homathko. With the wind fell the ice and snow until all trails were lost under the treacherous, windswept drifts.

If locked in by the snow, the family would be confined to the hut. If Miska were to die, it would be spring before the thaws allowed a proper Homathko burial ceremony. Cheela would have to be very cautious to keep herself well. She could not risk a fall or a broken bone, for little Toko and the old Miska had only Cheela to depend on until Piele returned.

Cheela remembered winters in Cumsack Creek when she woke to a white, silent, and empty world. At first, there was an unearthly, mysterious beauty to the winter world. With the first snow, the land was transformed overnight by a glittering mass of dazzling white. The tops of trees wore jeweled snowcaps and their boughs were garbed in frothy, lacy gowns of star-sprinkled beauty. On a clear, moonlit night, the wolves howled, and ice crystals glittered on the snow, and the river wound slowly in and out of the rocks, bypassing the pools and back eddies that turned to ice.

The silence of this world was so great, the stillness was so deep, and the beauty was so immense and unreal — it was magical for Cheela. But as the winter wore on, and the snow grew deeper, the struggle to exist always became greater. Thin, emaciated bodies of creatures of the wild froze to death. Like the animals of the forest, Cheela and her people could die just as easily when cold and hunger haunt the land. Cheela knew the margin between life and death was narrow when trapped in the snow beneath the ice fields of Homathko.

Piele had not come. And they would be trapped next to the Homathko for the winter.

"Why doesn't he come?" Cheela panicked. "What is keeping him? Is Miska right when she shakes her head at my words of hope?" Cheela sighed deeply, her whole body shaking. "No," she told herself. "Piele will be here in time to help us through the winter."

Then one day, before the first snow arrived, a man appeared. Far off, across the open meadow, they had seen a tall dark figure approaching.

"Piele!" Cheela cried. "At last he returns!"

She wished to race to meet him, to pour out her joy and welcome, but something checked her. An intuitive fear held her back. Cheela, Miska, and Toko waited and watched anxiously. It had to be Piele. She could not stand it, Cheela thought, if the strider were not Piele.

At long last the runner approached. It was not Piele. Cheela's heart sank. Toko looked to her, a question in his eyes. Only the old Miska sat unmoved. She had known that it could not be her son.

The messenger was Cheela's own brother, Talapus. She had wanted to see Piele so much that she hadn't recognized the form of her own brother. But the joy of reunion could not be. He had come to them, on the banks of the Homathko, swift as the wind, with news of Piele — frightening and dreadful news. And Cheela knew; when she looked upon his face, she knew.

Talapus told them, between breaths, of the misunderstanding and of the gifts. Piele and the others had been taken to the Cariboo where they had stood in the white man's courtroom.

It had taken several days to get here, he explained, but the morning he had left, the white officials had taken Piele and the others, and they had hanged them. With a rope around their necks they had hanged them until they were dead.

And they would bury them — like white men.

Cheela, shocked, tried to take it in. "Piele is dead!" Her mind screamed. "Piele is dead. Piele is never coming back."

Anger and agony seethed within her, making her feel faint. She screamed out — to object, for relief. They had killed her Piele and buried him — in the ground — in a country that was not his. What had gone wrong? Why had Piele not come? They could have survived in the wild without being caught. Why had someone not warned her sooner? Why? Why?

Miska simply wept, the sorrow in her body worse than the ache in her bones. Tears streamed down her brown and wrinkled face; her brown, sunken mouth quivered but her voice never spoke. Her heart was dead. Her heart was like winter.

Now Cheela sat staring into her stone, disbelieving. The same stone that had mesmerized her in another place, in another time. It lay on the floor of the hut, but Cheela did not see its mica glints. She was aware only of her grief, as deep as the sea and as high as the mountains and the canyon walls of Homathko, where all the trouble had started.

Piele was gone, Piele was dead. They were alone, desolate, and unprepared, and winter was hard upon them. As Cheela's tears ran, the first chill whispers of winter wind began to blow across *Xwe7xw's* glacial peaks. It felt, to Cheela, like the chill of death.

The years, like the river of Homathko, have rolled on, and the Bute Inlet winds have blown away the dark shadows of its unhappy past. The wagon road has long since returned to the wilderness from which it was taken. Bute Inlet remains as she was before the white man came, an unconquered land without a road, without a wagon, without a mule or a horse, without a train, without a rail—without the town that sprouted and died. Like a sleeping beauty, she awaits the magic touch of another dreamer, another Alfred Penderill Waddington.

Small mountain flowers, the pink Queen's cup, the creeping raspberry, and the alpine heather cover the ground and grow in cracks and crevices of rock where blood once spilled. Devil's club, salmon, and huckleberry bushes cover the forest floor where wagon wheels and mule teams once blazed a trail.

Across the glacial peaks, the cold winds still blow, and the moaning sound echoes Cheela's sobs. Cheela's ghost is said to haunt the hills and wander the plateaus and valleys of Homathko.

Homathko sleeps. *Xwe7xw* towers aloof, and has another name, that of the white man—Waddington.

There is a wind that wails in the winter night, like a lament for the shattered dreams and broken arrows left behind, for the dreams that were swept into British Columbian history by the turbulent waters of Homathko's river of tears.

Epilog

Alfred Penderill Waddington's dream of a railway did come true. His proposal was to build a transcontinental railroad from eastern Canada with its Pacific terminus at the head of Bute Inlet. He was prepared to begin in a small way by using a combined steamship and wagon road route, but later abandoned this idea in favor of the transcontinental railway idea, with a branch line to Bute Inlet.

Waddington spent the last years of his life trying to convince the authorities in Ottawa, where he died, of the need for his plan. And he succeeded, though he did not live to see it. In 1881, the government of Sir John A. Macdonald, in Ottawa, began construction of the Canadian Pacific Railway, which was to cross the continent and take the Burrard Inlet route.

Today, the highest mountain in British Columbia, Mount Waddington, stands as the tallest monument to one of the men who dreamed of a Canadian continental railway; the optimist, and the adventurer who was Alfred Waddington, the man sometimes remembered as one of the fathers of the Canadian Pacific Railway.

Further Reading

Dictionary of the Chinook Jargon or Indian Trade Language of the North Pacific Coast. Victoria: B.C. Stationary Co., 1887.

Fawcett, Edgar. *The Bute Inlet Massacre.* Public Archives of British Columbia.

Kennedy, Dorothy, and Bouchard, Randy. *Sliammon Life, Sliammon Lands.* Vancouver: Talonbooks, 1983.

Kirk, Ruth. *Wisdom of the Elders: Native Traditions on the Northwest Coast.* Toronto: Douglas and McIntyre, 1986.

McKelvie, Bruce. *Tales of Conflict.* Vancouver: Vancouver Province, 1949.

Morice, A. G. *History of the Northern Interior of British Columbia.* Toronto: William Briggs, 1905.

Nuffield, Edward W. *The Pacific Northwest.* Surrey: Hancock House Publishers Ltd., 1990.

Ormsby, Margaret A. *British Columbia: a History.* Toronto: The Macmillan Company of Canada, 1958.

Rothenberger, Mel. *The Chilcotin War.* Langley: Vanity Press, 1978.

Skelton, Robin. *They Call it the Cariboo.* Victoria: Sono Nis Press, 1980.

Waite, Donald E. *The Cariboo Gold Rush Story.* Surrey: Hancock House Publishers Ltd., 1988.

—— *The Fraser Canyon Story.* Surrey: Hancock House Publishers Ltd., 1988.

Walbran, Captain John T. *British Columbia Coast Names, 1592-1906: Their Origin and History.* Vancouver: J. J. Douglas, 1971.

Wayne, Kyra Petrovskaya. *Quest for Empire.* Surrey: Hancock House Publishers Ltd., 1986.